KING
ARTHUR'S
BRITAIN

◆

KING
ARTHUR'S
BRITAIN

◆

A PHOTOGRAPHIC ODYSSEY

John Matthews

Photographs by Michael J. Stead

BLANDFORD

A BLANDFORD BOOK

First published in the UK 1995 by Blandford
A Cassell Imprint
Cassell PLC, Wellington House
125 Strand, London WC2R 0BB

Distributed in the United States by Sterling Publishing Co., Inc.
387 Park Avenue South, New York, NY 10016–8810

Distributed in Australia by Capricorn Link (Australia) Pty Ltd
2/13 Carrington Road, Castle Hill, NSW 2154

**A Cataloguing-in-Publication Data entry for this title is
available from the British Library**

ISBN 0–7137–2528–1

Typeset by Keystroke, Jacaranda Lodge, Wolverhampton
Printed and bound in Slovenia by Printing House DELO – Tiskarna d.o.o.,
by arrangement with Korotan Ljubljana

◆ Previous page:
*Bamburgh Castle,
Northumberland.*

Dedication

*To Ari Berk,
who loves this land and feels its history
in his bones*

Acknowledgements

I am grateful to Michael Stead not only for the poetry and strength of his images – to my mind some of the best I have ever seen – but also for the suggestions for the inclusion of sites which would otherwise have been omitted, and for the wonderful and often hilarious account of his Travels in Search of Arthur. Thanks, too, to my editor, Stuart Booth, for suggesting the book in the first place and thereby giving me the opportunity to revisit some of the places I love for their Arthurian associations as much as for their intrinsic beauty and splendour.

CONTENTS

INTRODUCTION

◆

THE LAND OF ARTHUR

. . . that grey king whose name, a ghost,
Streams like a cloud, man-shaped,
from mountain peak,
and cleaves to cairn and cromlech still

Idylls of the King, Tennyson

Does the land wait the sleeping lord
or is the wasted land
that very lord who sleeps?

The Sleeping Lord, David Jones

'The King and the Land are one'

Merlin in John Boorman's film *Excalibur*

BRITAIN has two kinds of geography: the outer, visible one of hills, valleys, trees, rivers and plants; and the inner, mysterious, myth-haunted one which consists of places that are often no more than names, like Camelot, Camlan, the supposed site of Arthur's last battle, or Badon, the site of his greatest fight against the Saxons. Rivers of ink have been spilled by various commentators in their efforts to identify these places, many of which have remained undiscovered for the simple reason that they were never a part of this world at all, but belonged to the inner Britain of myth and legend. This is not to say that they never existed, only that the physical places ascribed to them are as often as not false.

However, since no one has yet devised a method of photographing the inner realms, and since the land itself contains a rich heritage of sites that bear the names of heroes long since gone, it seems appropriate still to draw upon the great book of the land to help us recall them.

The land remembers its heroes in many different ways: through story and song and folklore; but, most of all, through the places associated with them, which evoke particular tales. In Britain this is especially the case in the many places associated with the figure of Arthur. Britain has had many names in the past – some mythical, some historical – but one name which is inscribed into the land itself is the Land of Arthur, though you will not find it on maps or in guidebooks.

Geoffrey of Monmouth, the first writer to deal with Arthurian material in a connected and romantic fashion, described Britain as:

Britain, best of islands, is situated in the Western Ocean, between France and Ireland, being eight hundred miles long and two hundred broad. It produces everything that is useful to man, with a plenty that never fails. It abounds with all kinds of metal, and has plains of large extent, and hills fit for the finest tillage, the richness of whose soil affords variety of fruits in their proper seasons. It has also forests well stored with all kinds of wild beasts; in its lawns cattle find good change of pasture, and bees variety of flowers for honey. Under its lofty mountains lie green meadows pleasantly situated, in which the gentle murmurs of crystal springs gliding along clear channels, give those that pass an agreeable invitation to lie down on their banks and slumber. It is likewise well watered with lakes and rivers abounding with fish; and besides the narrow sea which is on the Southern coast towards France, there are three noble rivers, stretching out like three arms, namely, the Thames, the Severn, and the Humber; by which foreign commodities from all countries are brought into it.

History of the Kings of Britain,
Book I, Chapter 2

◆ Previous page:
Arthur's Quoit
St David's Head,
Wales.

This evokes later descriptions of the otherworldly island of Avalon where, in Tennyson's famous lines:

> . . . falls not hail, or rain, or any
>   snow,
> Nor ever wind blows loudly;
>   but it lies
> Deep meadow'd, happy, fair with
>   orchard lawns
> And bowery hollows crown'd with
>   summer sea.

The Passing of Arthur

Place-names which recall Arthur's presence abound, including Arthur's Seat, Arthur's O'on, King Arthur's Cups and Saucers, Arthur's Quoit (in fact there are dozens of these) and several Arthur's Graves. Others, such as Glastonbury Tor and Cadbury Camp in Somerset, Dozemary Pool and Tintagel Castle in Cornwall, and Sewingshields Crag and Richmond Castle in Yorkshire, resound with tales that bind them inextricably to the story of the Matter of Britain, irrespective of historicity or proof.

Of course, this is as it should be: one should not go looking for the actual stones of Camelot, any more than we should expect to find the stone in which Arthur's first sword was embedded. Instead, we find the print of Arthur's hound, Cafal, in a stone in Wales, or the river or pool into which Excalibur was consigned when the king no longer had a use for it.

It may be asked why Arthur should be remembered in this way: what did he do to distinguish himself in such a way that he became the *genius loci* of Britain?

It is not possible to state, with any final certainty, whether or not such a person called Arthur ever lived. If he did, he most certainly was not a king, did not wear shining armour, and in all probability was not accompanied by a band of noble knights who sat together at a round table. It is more likely that Arthur was a sixth-century war-lord who helped bind together the Celtic peoples of Britain into a force strong enough to repulse the invasion of the Saxons, Angles and Jutes which was then taking place. Arthur held the Celts together long enough for their enemies to identify them as settlers rather than invaders, and thus to found the beginnings of the English race.

Whatever the truth of the matter, Arthur became a central figure in what we might call the mythological, or inner, story of Britain. Earlier memories of a shadowy Celtic deity, called perhaps Arth or Arthyr, and of possibly several other heroes with the same name, coalesced into the figure we know today. Because most of the stories were written down in the Middle Ages – from the eleventh to the end of the fifteenth centuries – the characters, dress, morals and motivation are of that time.

The recording of various sites associated with Arthur seems to have begun almost as soon as his departure from the lands of men into the Otherworld (see below). Nennius, one of the earliest writers to mention Arthur whose work has survived, lists a number of 'Wonders of the Island of Britain', including:

There is another wonder in the country called Builth. There is a heap of stones there, and one of the stones placed on top of the pile has the footprint of a dog on it. When he hunted the Twrch Trwyth, Cafal, the warrior Arthur's hound, impressed his footprint on the stone, and Arthur later brought together the pile of stones, under the stone in which was his dog's footprint, and it is called Carn Cafal. Men come and take the stone in their hands for the space of a day and a night, and on the morrow it is found upon the stone pile.

trans. J. Morris

and:

There is another wonder in the country called Ergyng. There is a tomb there by a spring, called Llygad Amr; the name of the man who is buried in the tomb was Amr. He was the son of the warrior Arthur, and he killed him there and buried him. Men come to measure the tomb, and it is sometimes six feet long, sometimes nine, sometimes twelve, sometimes fifteen. At whatever measure you measure it on one occasion, you never find it again the same measure, and I have tried it myself.

trans. J. Morris

A photograph of the stone containing the print of Arthur's *horse* can be found on page 89. Whether it is really the same one seen by Nennius and later on by Gerald of Wales remains to be seen. Gerald was that indefatigable medieval traveller and raconteur whose *Journey Through Wales* and *Description of Wales* give a fascinating insight into the people, as well as the traditions, of the country in the twelfth century. Gerald gives us one of the best and most complete descriptions of the discovery of Arthur's 'grave' at Glastonbury in about 1191.

In our own lifetime Arthur's body was discovered at Glastonbury, although the legends have always encouraged us to believe that there was something otherworldly about his ending, that he had resisted death and had been spirited away to some far-distant spot. The body was hidden deep in the earth in a hollowed-out oak-bole and between two stone pyramids which had been set up long ago in the churchyard there. They carried it into the church with every mark of honour and buried it decently there in a marble tomb.

De Principis Instructionae, trans. L. Thorpe

Much had been written about this discovery. To this day a plaque with the inscription describing this to be the grave of Arthur can still be seen in the grounds of Glastonbury Abbey (see page 109), though there is no real evidence as to its authenticity. There are those who believe that this was indeed the place where Arthur's remains were interred, but scholarly opinion generally believes that the whole business was a fraud, invented by the monks of Glastonbury to enable them to raise funds to rebuild the abbey, which had been partly destroyed by fire a few years before. Perhaps it is best to adopt the stance of the early Welsh poet who wrote, in a collection of gnomic verses called 'The Stanzas of the Graves':

> A grave for March,
> a grave for Gwgawn
> of the Bloody Sword.
> Not wise the thought,
> a grave for Arthur.

Britain has always been a myth-haunted place. It has known many heroes and has had many names: Albion (after a giant who dwelled here before recorded history); Clas Myrddin or Merlin's Enclosure (after the great Welsh enchanter); Logres, deriving from the Welsh word for England which later became conflated with the Old French *l'orgelluse*, to give us 'The Proud Land'; and throughout the Celtic myths collected under the title of *The Mabinogion* as The Island of the Mighty. It was believed by many who did not live on its shores to be the actual Otherworld, and stories are told of the god Apollo visiting it and of another god, Kronos, being buried beneath it. Yet it is Arthur's presence that dominates it, and it is his internment in the Land itself – where he sleeps until the time when his country calls out to him again – that makes Britain his.

The Roman author Plutarch, in the *De Defectu Oraculorum* (*The Death of Oracles*), talks of:

. . . an island in which Kronos is imprisoned with Briareus keeping guard over him as he sleeps; for, as they put it, sleep is the bond forged for Kronos. They add that around him are many deities, his henchmen and attendants.

De Defectu, XVIII

Just why Kronos should have been represented as lying beneath an island off the shores of Britain is less easy to explain. E. K. Chambers suggests that the report may originally have described the Celtic god Curnunnos, which sounds not unlike Kronos. While this may be doubtful, it is interesting to note that the figure who guards him – 'Briareus' – can be shown to be derived from 'Barinthus' who appears in Geoffrey of Monmouth's *Life of Merlin*. He was a navigator who knew the ways of the stars and planets well and who, with the bard Taliesin, guided the boat carrying the wounded Arthur across the water to the Island of Avalon.

In Greek myth, of course, Kronos is banished and bound by his son Zeus (whom he had tried to consume), whereas Arthur's reason for resting beneath the land is very different. None the less, the parallels are striking enough to suggest that the ancient British story was reinterpreted by Plutarch in terms which his readers could understand. If this is the case, then the story of a king or some other mighty figure sleeping beneath the earth is far older than the myths of Arthur, which suggests that his name was substituted for a more ancient figure who is no longer remembered.

The idea that Arthur is asleep beneath various hills and mountains throughout Britain derives, in part at least, from the ancient concept of kingship which represented the king as intimately connected to the land. In Ireland, in particular, this resulted in stories where the would-be king encountered the figure of Eriu, the personification of Ireland, and either went through a form of marriage or cohabited with her before he could be judged fit to rule the land. In Arthurian myth, this figure has become fragmented into a number of forms with a surprising number of names; nevertheless, she represents the 'sovereignty' of Britain, and Arthur (as represented by his knights) undergoes a long series of trials intended to test not only his individual courage, but also his ability to rule the kingdom. Thus Gawain, who represents Arthur on a number of occasions, undergoes the tests of the Beheading Game and marriage to the Loathly Lady, each of which reprises the ancient question of the king's right to rule over the land. In the former, the Green Knight, a fearsome otherworldly figure, enters the court at Christmas and challenges anyone to an exchange of blows. Gawain, accepting on behalf of Arthur, cuts off the intruder's head, only to see him raise it by the hair and hear it speak of another meeting in a year's time. Of course, Gawain succeeds, with the help of magic and his own courage, and survives to wed the Loathly Lady – in a borrowing from the older story of the king's wedding to the Land, Gawain wins both his life and the love of the transformed hag who becomes his beautiful wife. The setting for the first of these stories may be Wetton Mill in Staffordshire (see page 70).

In the Grail story – perhaps the greatest of the many Arthurian epics – the Quest is undertaken not only to discover the mystic cup or cauldron, but also to heal the Waste Land, a tract of country surrounding the castle of the Grail which is specifically said to be barren and desolate because its king suffers from an unhealing wound. In other words, since the king is sick, the land is also sick. It is clear that at one time this theme extended to Arthur himself, so that it is he who is wounded and his land – Britain itself – which requires healing. This is simply a logical extension of the ideas which put forward the theory that the king and the land are so closely related that what affects one is expressed physically in the other.

At the end of his story, Arthur does not die as other men do, but is taken to the otherwordly Isle of Avalon, ruled over by the Ladies of the Lake. There, we learn, he will be healed of his wounds and await the time when he is called back into the mundane world to help his country. Thereafter, he is pictured as waiting, sometimes asleep like Kronos on his golden rock, while Avalon becomes synonymous with the land of Britain itself.

I hope this book will encourage other explorers to set off in search of Arthur's Britain, because there are still sites waiting to be rediscovered, many of them referred to only in local folklore. I am always interested in hearing of any such places which I may have missed in my own wanderings, for indeed:

> She is not any common earth,
>   Water or wood or air,
> But Merlin's Isle of Gramarye
>   Where you and I will fare.
>
> A. E. Housman

John Matthews
Oxford

MAP OF ARTHURIAN SITES IN BRITAIN

Lothian

Stirling (The King's Knot)

Edinburgh
(Arthur's Seat)

Eildon Hills

Bamburgh Castle

Drumelzier
(Merlin's Grave)

R. Tweed

Alnwick Castle

Hart Fell

Arfderydd

Hadrian's Wall

Sewingshields

Lochmaben

Clochmabenstane

Kings Crags
and Queens Crags

Mote of Mark

Carlisle

Pendragon Castle

Richmond Castle

Anglesey

Maen Chwyf

Ogof Arthur

Llyn Dinas

Chester

Alderley Edge
(Merlin's Rock)

Arthur's Quoit

Dinas Emrys

Dinas Bran

Wetton Mill

Bardsey Island

Cors-y-gedol

Llyn Barfog

Wales

Logres

Pentre Ifan

Preselly Mountains

Cerrig Meibion Arthur

Carmarthen

Arthur's Cave

(The Tor, The Abbey,
Wearyall Hill, Chalice Well)

Caerleon

St. Govan's Chapel

Bristol Channel

Bath

R. Thames

Liddington Castle

Glastonbury

Marlborough (Merlin's Pyramid)

Stonehenge

St. Nechtan's Kieve

Devon

Roche Rock

Cadbury Castle

Winchester
(Round Table)

Slaughter Bridge

King Arthur's Bed

Badbury Rings

Tintagel Castle
& Merlin's Cave

Dozemary Pool

Maiden Castle

St. Michael's Mount

Castle Dore

Cornwall

Trethevy Quoit

Chapel Point

The Tristan Stone

Looe Pool

To Lyonesse (The Scilly Isles)

1

MERLIN AND THE BIRTH OF ARTHUR

A lonely man, his head among the stars
Walks on the clean sand white beside the sea;
Merlin, the lonely man of Camelot,
Who left King Arthur and the tournaments
And decorous garlands and the sight of man
Dear to him, yea! the knights and pageantry
To walk beside the waves that curl in foam
And sparkling splendour round him.

Thomas Caldecot Chubb

THE story begins with Merlin, who was there to usher in the age of Arthur with all its attendant marvels. He prophesied the coming of the new king and saw to it that through the miracle of the Sword in the Stone he was recognized and crowned with all the pomp and circumstance of the time. So it is right to begin our exploration of Arthur's Britain with some of the places to which the name Merlin has become attached.

We first hear of him as a wonderful child, brought before the tyrant Vortigern on the hill called Dinas Emrys (see page 31), prophesying the many ages to come until the end of time itself. From here onwards, he becomes an important figure in the Arthurian tradition, a prime mover who helps to establish the youthful Arthur as king and who guides and instructs him throughout the first years of his reign.

However, perhaps because having an omniscient wizard at his side would have made things too easy for Arthur, Merlin is taken out of the picture in a fashion as mysterious as his coming. According to some versions, he becomes enamoured of Nimue, one of the Ladies of the Lake. Apparently sick of being pursued by the aged enchanter, she uses her wiles to gain access to Merlin's secrets to turn them against him; using them to shut him away, either beneath a great rock, in a thorn-bush or even in a tower of glass.

◆ Previous page:
Dinas Emrys,
Gwynedd,
North Wales.

The latter gives us a possible clue to Merlin's real end.

In his *Vita Merlini* (*Life of Merlin*), Geoffrey of Monmouth recounts an alternative version of the story: the wise man retires voluntarily to a great observatory, with 70 windows, hidden deep within the woods. The observatory is built for him by his sister Ganeida. It is possible that from this small seed came the later tale of the wise magician duped and then ensorcelled by the fairy Nimue. The truth seems to be that Merlin grew weary of the ways of humankind (he himself is said to be the offspring of a liaison between a fairy and a mortal woman) and to have retired to his observatory, there to watch the circling of the stars and read the future in which he would – one day – play a part once more.

The literary origins of Merlin are as obscure as his legendary nascence. A group of poems attributed to a sixth-century bard named Myrddin has been identified as his, though they may well be the works of another man: a semi-historical king of the Southern Cymry (Welsh) whose history has become inextricably mixed with that of his more famous namesake. The English medieval work which bears his name has Merlin appearing one last time, after his so-called 'imprisonment' by Nimue, to the wandering Sir Gawain, who reports that his last words are:

Me shall you never more see, though it grieves me sorely that I may do no other; and when you are departed from hence, I shall never speak with you again, nor with any other, save only with my leave: for never man shall have power to come hither for any reason. Nor from hence may I come out, nor ever shall I come out, for in all the world is not so strong a prison as this where I am, and it is neither made of iron, or timber, or stone, but rather of air alone, by enchantment so strong that it will never be undone while the world endures. Nor may I come out, or anyone enter, save she that enclosed me here, who bears me company when she likes, and goes hence when she likes.

The English Merlin, ed. H. B. Wheatley

But it is in another medieval work, the *Didot Perceval* by an unknown author, that Merlin best describes his own fate:

And then Merlin . . . told them . . . that he would not be able to die before the end of the world; [but that he wished] 'to make a lodging outside . . . and to dwell there and . . . prophesy . . . And all those who will see my lodging will name it the *esplumoir* (or moulting cage) of Merlin'.

trans. D. Skeels

It seems somehow appropriate for the old wise man to end thus, with a pun: the moulting cage is a place where hawks, of which the merlin is one, are put when they are losing their old feathers and growing a new plumage. The *esplumoir* (the exact meaning of which is obscure) is thus a place where the enchanter can rest and undergo a different kind of apotheosis, from which he will someday emerge to play his part once again in the affairs of humankind.

Tintagel

◆

Cornwall

◄ A fire which burned the grass and topsoil from the surface of the island in 1993 revealed evidence of more extensive building and occupation than had been suspected, suggesting that the site was of far greater importance than previous excavations had shown.

Perhaps the most familiar of all the sites associated with Arthur. Local tradition, founded largely on the writings of Geoffrey of Monmouth in his twelfth-century *History of the Kings of Britain*, claims this as the birthplace of Arthur, from where Merlin took him to be fostered in secret. The dramatic ruins of the castle, dating from the twelfth to thirteenth centuries, are too late to have anything to do with the real Arthur. None the less, they are responsible for a good deal of romantic inspiration. The anonymous medieval writer of *The Folie Tristan* said that the castle was built by giants and that it used to vanish twice a year – at midwinter and again at midsummer. Thomas Hardy visited and later drew the castle from memory, re-instating its medieval might. Sir Arnold Bax (1883–1953) composed a wonderful tone-poem evoking the majesty and mystery of the place in 1917; to listen to it is to hear the waves crashing against the rocks below the castle.

A much earlier monastic site on the island promontory behind the castle dates from a time more or less contemporary with Arthur. More recent discoveries, following excavations in 1994, indicate that it may have been a Celtic site of some importance. The most recent thinking suggests that there may well be something in the legends surrounding the place.

▶ *The sea rushes into this tiny inlet at high tides, effectively cutting off the promontory and turning it into an island.*

Merlin's Cave

◆

Cornwall

Tennyson made this place famous in his *Idylls of the King* when he described waves bringing the infant Arthur to the shore, where he was plucked out by Merlin and carried to safety. Local legend has long associated this cave – which fills with water at every high tide – with the great enchanter. It is certainly a place of considerable atmosphere, where one might indeed expect to see Merlin approaching, with his shining staff held up to illuminate the darkness of the cave. It is now mostly the haunt of scuba-divers in search of shells and fossils.

▶ *The rocks of Tintagel cliffs loom out over the entrance to Merlin's Cave, making it a dark and gloomy place – until, that is, the sun finds its way in through a crack in the rocks, briefly illuminating it.*

Pendragon Castle

◆

Cumbria

◀ *The possible site of the castle traditionally believed to have belonged to King Arthur's father, Uther Pendragon.*

The ruins which crown this hill among the moors of Mallerstang, near Kirkby Stephen, are said to have once belonged to Uther Pendragon, Arthur's father in the legends. There seem little grounds for believing this, because the castle is, in fact, a medieval building which belonged to Hugh de Morville, one of the murderers of Thomas à Becket. There may be the remains of earlier fortifications, however, and there is also local legend which tells how Uther tried to divert the nearby River Eden to fill a moat around the hill. A rhyme commemorates this:

> *Let Uther Pendragon do what he can.*
> *Eden will run where Eden ran.*

What may possibly be the outlines of trenches can still be seen around the base of the hill, suggesting the veracity of this story. References to a character named Uther (or Gorlasser) exist in early Welsh tradition, though nothing is known of him other than the legend which makes him the father of the future king.

Bardsey Island

◆

Gwynedd, North Wales

Set in the sea off the coast of Wales, local legend tells that this was the island to which Merlin retired to live in his observatory. Another story says that here are hidden the Thirteen Treasures of the Island of Britain, including the Cauldron of Diwrnach the Giant, the Whetstone of Tudglyd, and Arthur's Mantle of Invisibility. Merlin is said to be their guardian.

Earlier references describe the island (then called Ynys Enlli) as the site of a Celtic monastery founded in 516 by a Breton prince named Cadfan. Remains of a thirteenth-century Augustinian foundation dedicated to St Mary still stand in the centre of the island. The island is also said to be the burial site of 20,000 saints, making it a very holy place indeed. Three pilgrimages here in the Middle Ages were considered the equal of a visit to Rome. The island was believed to be an extremely healthy spot where, as the medieval chronicler Giraldus Cambrensis notes, 'no one dies except from old age'.

▶ *The distant hump of Bardsey rises from the sea, framed by the inhospitable rocks of the Lleyn peninsula. It is easy to see why this wild and desolate spot acquired its magical associations.*

▶ *It is believed that Bardsey was once joined to the mainland, when it formed part of the kingdom of Gwyddno Garanhir. According to legend, this kingdom was overwhelmed by a great tidal wave in the sixth century.*

Dinas Emrys

◆

Gwynedd, North Wales

According to tradition, Vortigern, the usurping King of Britain in the fifth century, fled to this place. He was pursued by the Saxon mercenaries he had invited to help him against the invading Picts and Scoti. Vortigern tried to build a fortress on the hilltop, but it kept falling down as soon as his masons had built it. Consulting his wizards, he was told that only the blood of a child without a father, spilled upon the stones, would enable the fortress to stand. Merlin (then known as Emrys) fitted the bill. When he was brought before Vortigern, he challenged the king's advisers to disclose the real reason why the fortress would not stand. He then revealed the presence of two dragons, imprisoned in a stone coffin at the bottom of an underground lake beneath the crest. This proved correct and the dragons were set free to fight in the air above the hill. Merlin, prophesying the death of Vortigern, then gave vent to his first and greatest visions, many of which were later recorded by Geoffrey of Monmouth, so they are still extant. The remains of a tower can be seen on the hilltop and though they seem to be medieval rather than Dark-Age, they lend credence to the story.

Other legends speak of Merlin's treasure – a golden vessel and a golden chair – buried somewhere beneath the hill, awaiting discovery by a golden-haired youth.

Llyn Dinas

◆

Gwynedd, North Wales

This still pool of water reflects the shape of nearby Dinas Emrys and it is said to have been the site of a long-ago battle between Owein, one of Arthur's greatest warriors, and a giant. Here, also, in a secret place, the usurper-king Vortigern is supposed to have hidden the throne of Britain beneath a great stone. This may be in part a memory of Merlin's treasure, which is apparently buried beneath the nearby hill (see page 31).

◄ *One of the many mysterious pools or lakes which have associations with Arthur and his heroes*

Stonehenge

◆

Wiltshire

Among the many legends connected with this famous site is one telling of its construction by Merlin. He was asked by Arthur's father, King Uther Pendragon, to construct a fitting memorial for his brother Ambrosius and the war-lords of Britain felled by Saxon treachery in the massacre known as the Night of the Long Knives. Merlin journeyed to Ireland in search of the fabled Giant's Dance, a circle of huge stones which were believed to possess curative properties if water in which they had been washed was used to bathe the sick. After a great battle, Merlin conveyed the stones by magic to the shore of sea, then floated them on rafts across to Britain and set them up on the plain near Salisbury. It has been suggested that this story may contain a distant memory of the method by which the ancient blue-stones, quarried in the Prescelly Mountains far to the north, were brought by sea to the mouth of the River Avon and then taken inland on huge wooden rollers to their present site. Despite numerous theories, which claim Stonehenge to be anything from an ancient observatory to a Druid temple, little is known about the true origin or purpose of this mighty circle of stones.

Alderley Edge

◆

Cheshire

According to a local tradition, in the ground below the great outcrop of sandstone, known as the Edge, there is a cave in which Arthur and his knights lie sleeping. The story goes that a farmer was on his way to market at the nearby town of Macclesfield when he was stopped by an old man who offered to buy the white horse he was planning to sell. Refusing a low offer, the farmer rode on. Despite much interest, no one bought his horse at the market. On the way back, the same mysterious man appeared and this time the farmer accepted his offer. Leading him to the hillside, the old man laid a hand on some rocks, which opened to reveal iron gates at an entrance into the hill. Within the hill, the astonished farmer saw the great king and his knights, together with their mounts, asleep in a vast cavern. The horse was for one of the knights, and the farmer received a bag of gold for it before he fled, hearing the gates clang shut behind him.

▶ *Merlin's rock, Alderley. Close by is a mossy outcrop from which water drips into a small stone trough. Above it, a bearded, weather-beaten face can be discerned. Under it is written, in letters carved more recently: Drink of this and take thy fill, for the water falls by the wizard's will.*

◄ *This is where Arthur and his knights are believed to be sleeping beneath the hill. They will awaken and return to help beleaguered Britain in desperate times.*

Hart Fell

◆

Dumfries and Galloway, Scotland

Here, in the centre of an area rich in sites associated with Merlin, lies a precipitous valley leading to what one of the leading authorities on Merlin, Nikolai Tolstoy, has identified as the cave where the celebrated sage took refuge after the Battle of Arfderydd. According to Geoffrey of Monmouth's *Vita Merlini*, it was here that he went mad and fled into the mountains. Hart Fell lies in the centre of what was once the extensive Forest of Celyddon, where, once again, tradition places Merlin in his period of inspired madness. In the medieval romance of *Fergus of Galloway* by Guillaume le Clerc (Everyman, 1993) there is a description of its hero's journey from the Moat of Liddel to the summit of the Black Mountain, where Merlin is again to be found. This fits so well with the local landscape as to be virtually conclusive in identifying the site with Merlin's refuge.

▶ *View towards the summit of Arthur's Mount, also called the Black Mountain. Merlin's cave lies hidden among the tumbled stones at the foot of Hart Fell.*

◀ *The view from Hart Fell. The great Forest of Celyddon once covered this area and a black knight lingered nearby to challenge all who approached.*

A chalebate spring, containing iron salts with proven curative properties, rises in the hills and runs down the valley where Merlin's cave is situated. Nikolai Tolstoy believes that the name *fons galabes* (Fountain of Galabes?), a spring associated with Merlin by Geoffrey of Monmouth in his twelfth-century *The History of the Kings of Britain*, may have been a corruption of *fons chalybs*. More than one medieval story associates Merlin with a healing spring: for example, the Fountain of Barenton in the forest of Broceliande in Brittany. It is certainly possible that a story of a mad prophet in a cave in the fells, who was later healed by drinking the curative waters of a spring, may have become attached to the area around Hart Fell by a story-teller whose work only survived in the memory of medieval romance writers.

▶ *Up this steep valley lies the way to the cave thought to have been Merlin's refuge after he went mad at the Battle of Arfderydd, in which both friends and relatives perished. The supposed site of the battle lies only 48 km (30 miles) to the south-east.*

Merlin's Grave

Dumbarton, Scotland

Like Arthur, Merlin has many 'graves' scattered across the countryside, with several areas eager to claim his bones. This site lies at the junction of Powsail burn and the River Tweed. A prophecy attributed to the Scots seer, Thomas the Rhymer, has it that:

When Tweed and Pausayl meet
at Merlin's Grave
Scotland and England shall
one monarch have.

This prediction was seen to come true in 1603, when the Powsail overflowed its banks and merged with the Tweed. That same year James VI of Scotland was crowned James I of England, uniting both countries under a single monarch.

A nearby hill is named Drumelzier, which may be derived from 'Dunmeller' (Merlin's Hill). Other local references to Merlin include Merlindale, a hamlet immediately to the west of Drumelzier, and Stobo Kirk, where a church window remembers the healing of Merlin by St Kentigern (Mungo), who is believed to have cured him with water from a local spring.

◄ Far left: *In the shade of this tree lies the possible site of Merlin's grave. A small cairn of stones marks the spot where the renowned seer is believed to be buried.*

Merlin's Pyramid

◆

Marlborough, Wiltshire

Far to the south lies another claimant for the grave of Merlin. Half-hidden now among trees and enclosed within the grounds of Marlborough College, little can be seen of the original site. However, an eighteenth-century engraving shows a large terraced mound not unlike Silbury Hill in appearance. A medieval castle once stood on its summit, but the mound itself is probably older. Seventeenth-century excavators, who altered the shape of the mound to meet the current fashion in landscaping, are believed to have found Roman coins there, which suggests a lengthy period of occupation.

The association with Merlin seems to derive from the thirteenth century, when a poem by Alexander Neckham, the Abbot of Cirencester, states that 'Merlin's Tumulus gave you your name, Merleburgia', which led to a widespread belief in a Merlin connection with the area. In fact, coins from the period of William the Conqueror indicate that the town was called 'Maerlebi' or 'Maerliber' even in this time, whereas Geoffrey of Monmouth was the first to spell Merlin in this way almost 200 years later; before then it had been spelt with a double 'd' – Myrddin. It is meant to have been changed because of its similarity with the French *merde*!

2

THE ROUND TABLE

Full fifteen years, and more, were sped;
Each brought new wreaths to
Arthur's head.
Twelve Bloody fields, with glory fought,
The Saxons to subjection brought;
Rython, the mighty giant slain
By his good brand, relieved Bretagne:
The Pictish Gillamore in flight,
And Roman Lucius, own'd his might;
And wide were through the
world renown'd
The glories of his Table Round.

Sir Walter Scott

PERHAPS the most famous institution of its kind is the Round Table, yet its origins are as shadowy as Arthur's. It is first mentioned in the writing of a twelfth-century monk named Robert Wace, born in Jersey around 1100. He translated Geoffrey of Monmouth's Latin *History of the Kings of Britain* into Norman French, adding various details in the process, among them the Round Table. Wace describes its foundation as follows:

Arthur never heard speak of a knight in praise, but he caused him to be numbered in his household . . . Because of these noble lords about his hall, of whom each knight pained himself to be hardiest champion, and none would count him the least praiseworthy, Arthur made the Round Table, so reputed of the Britons. This Round Table was ordained by Arthur that when his fair fellowship sat to meet their chairs should be high alike, their service equal, and none before or after his comrade. Thus no man could boast that he was above his fellow, for all alike were gathered around the board, and none were alien at the breaking of Arthur's bread.

Wace: Roman de Brut, trans. Eugene Mason

From here on the table became increasingly prominent in the romances that continued to be written about Arthur and his knights throughout the Middle Ages. By the time Sir Thomas Malory wrote his great book *Le Morte d'Arthur* in the fifteenth century, the mythology of the Round Table was firmly in place. The knights who joined the fellowship swore an oath before a mighty Christian monarch:

. . . never to do outrage or murder, and always to flee treason; also, by no means to be cruel, but to give mercy to them that asked mercy, upon pain of forfeiture of their worship and lordship of King Arthur forevermore; and always to do ladies, damosels, and gentlewomen succour, upon pain of death. Also, that no man take battles in a wrongful quarrel for no law, nor for world's goods. Unto this were all the knights sworn of the Round Table, both old and young. And every year were they sworn at the high feast of Pentecost.

Le Morte d'Arthur, Book III, Chapter 15

The table itself, from its humble beginnings in Wace's *Roman de Brut*, had developed almost cosmic proportions, being made round 'in likeness of the world' by no lesser person than Merlin himself; while to Arthur's court came knights from all over the world, seeking to become part of the fabled Fellowship of the Round Table. Their adventures took them to many parts of the land, as they rode 'overthwart and endlong' through the forest of adventure into shadowy valleys where lurked strange creatures, or across streams and rivers where Black Knights waited at the fording places ready to challenge all comers.

◆ Previous page: *Alnwick Castle, Northumberland.*

Much of this landscape was imaginary, a metaphor of the Quest itself; but occasionally real places entered into the picture and acquired their own associations. The Round Table itself was to be seen at Winchester (believed by some to be the site of Camelot). Indeed, a table still hangs there to this day (see page 64), though it is no older than the Tudor period, long after the Age of Arthur. Other sites had their own romantic traditions. Bamburgh Castle was widely believed to be the home of Sir Lancelot, Arthur's bravest knight – and the lover of his queen. Wetton Mill, in Staffordshire (see page 70), was thought to be the original site of the Green Knight's chapel, where the fearsome challenger of Arthur's knights lay in wait, sharpening his giant axe on the rocks near by. Castle Dore, in Cornwall, or Maiden Castle, in Dorset, became the home of King Mark, a mean-spirited man whose beautiful wife, Iseult, fell in love with the king's nephew, Tristan, who, when captured by his uncle's men, leapt to safety from the window of a building on Roche Rock, in Cornwall (see page 55). Cadbury Castle, in Somerset (see page 50), was for years believed to be the original site of Camelot. Excavations in the 1960s failed to prove the matter conclusively, but went some way towards convincing the world that it might be so.

In these and the other sites shown here, the spirit of the Round Table lives on, and it is easy to feel that, if one only turned around quickly enough, one might still catch a glimpse of one of the knights, preparing to do battle on behalf of a distressed lady.

Cadbury Castle

Somerset

▲ *The powerful bulk of the fort on Cadbury Hill rises above the flat Somerset plain. If this was the original site of Camelot, it would have been famed throughout most of southern Britain in Arthur's time.*

▶ *Trees now cloak the sides of Cadbury Camp, yet its imposing bank-and-ditch ramparts would have presented a formidable obstacle to attackers trying to climb it in the face of a determined defence from above.*

Cadbury has been associated with Arthur since at least the sixteenth century, when the distinguished antiquarian John Leland described it in his account of ancient British history. He wrote: 'At the very south end of the church of South-Cadbyri standeth Camallate, sometime a famous town or castle . . . The people can tell nothing there but that they have heard say Arthur much resorted to Camalat . . .' Camallate or Camalat is, of course, Camelot, the famed citadel of Arthur where the Round Table was housed and from where the Fellowship of Knights rode forth in search of adventure and wrongs to right. Whether the association of Cadbury is a genuine one has been hotly disputed for a number of years. There are those who think that Leland invented the connection from the close-lying place-names of Queen Camel and West Camel; others would have us believe the identification a true one. Certainly, the archaeological investigation which took place there in the 1960s indicated that the hill, which is really an Iron-Age camp, was re-fortified with extensive earth and timber defences during the crucial period of the sixth century when Arthur is believed to have flourished. The foundations of an extensive timbered hall, and what appear to be the beginnings of an unfinished church, add further to the speculation, as does the closeness of the site to Glastonbury Tor (see page 113). A causeway, known as King Arthur's Hunting Track, links the two sites, and a plethora of local legends support the Arthurian connection. As late as the nineteenth century, when a group of Victorian 'archaeologists' came to investigate the stories clustering about the hill, a local man asked if they had 'come to dig up the king'. Folklore still retains a memory of Arthur and his knights sleeping under the hill. It is said that if one leaves a silver coin with one's horse on Midsummer's Eve, the horse will be found to be re-shod in the morning.

Castle Dore

◆

Cornwall

Like the hill-fort at Cadbury (see page 50), this Iron-Age fortress shows little of its former glory, save for the massive banks and ditches which were its chief line of defence. Again, like Cadbury, it was re-fortified in the sixth century, it is said, by a prince named Cynfawr, who is better remembered as King Mark, husband to the ill-fated Queen Iseult who was loved by Mark's nephew Tristan. In fact, this famous love-story was probably set in Scotland, or at least much further north than Castle Dore, but local traditions insist that this was the site of Mark's 'castle'. A possible reason for this may have been that a real lord of the area (one suggestion is the Roman governor of the area, Marcus Cunomorus) may have had a son named Tristan or Drustan, and that story-tellers made the ensuing connection. Whatever the truth, the site still claims a powerful feeling of association with the tale of the doomed lovers.

Roche Rock

◆

Cornwall

The story of the doomed love of Tristan and Iseult is one of the most famous and much loved subjects of the medieval romancers who created the vast epics of Arthurian literature. Tristan was King Mark's nephew who, having been sent to fetch his uncle's bride-to-be from Ireland, accidentally shared a love potion with her so that the two fell hopelessly in love. Thereafter, their lives were lived in a series of furtive trysts, while they both sought to escape the traps laid for them by the suspicious Mark. In the end, Tristan met his death and Iseult, unable to live without him, followed soon after.

A number of sites in and around Cornwall and the far north commemorate this tragic tale. One of the most spectacular is Roche Rock, a massive outcrop of granite, rising from a landscape ruined by clay mining, on which is perched the remains of a fifteenth century chapel. A contemporary theory, first advanced by E. M. R. Ditmas in her study of the topography of the Tristan legend, suggests that this may have been the site of the hermit Ogrin's chapel, where the lovers, having escaped from King Mark, found temporary refuge. The medieval poet Beroul, who wrote one of the earliest versions of the story, appears to display an intimate knowledge of the Cornish landscape, and his description of Ogrin's chapel certainly bears a more than passing resemblance to Roche Rock.

A later version of the story speaks of Tristan's escape from Mark's soldiers – who had locked him in a cell within another chapel – by jumping from the window down on to some perilous rocks. Such a feat would not be beyond an athletic man, though the result might well be fatal. Near by, at Chapel Point, overlooking the sea near Mevagissey, is the supposed site of 'Tristan's Leap', but a far more likely site would seem to be Roche Rock, where such a dramatic escape would have stayed in the minds of local story-tellers and might well have become known to one of the authors of the early Tristan story.

◄ A dangerous, winding way over broken rocks leads up to the remains of the tiny chapel. Local tradition insists that there were hermits here long before the Middle Ages.

◀ *The landscape glimpsed from within the ruins of the fifteenth-century chapel bears little resemblance to the one the Hermit Ogrin or, indeed, the fugitive lovers would have seen; generations of clay mining have ruined it for ever.*

The Mote of Mark

◆

Dumfries and Galloway, Scotland

Alternative versions of the Tristan and Iseult story see it as taking place in the north of Britain rather than in Cornwall. A number of sites echo this, foremost among them being the Mote of Mark, near Rockliffe on the southern coast of Scotland, which makes an interesting variation on the alternative site at Castle Dore (see page 52) in Cornwall. The argument turns upon the question of whether the original characters of the story, who may well have existed, originated from the north or south of the country. According to one set of arguments, the names Drustan (Tristan) and March (Mark) actually originate in Scotland, and are of Pictish origin. This has the effect of pushing the story back to a much earlier era than that of Arthur, possibly by as much as 100 years. The more popular theory places the entire scheme of events in Cornwall, with Mark's palace at Castle Dore and a plethora of lesser sites bearing the name of Tristan.

▶ *This formidable crag may have been the home of a Northern lord whose story became attached to that of Tristan and Iseult.*

▶ *A memorial to the hero Tristan stands beside the road near the Cornish town of Fowey. If it ever marked the grave of the man whose name appears on it, it no longer does so, because successive relocations over the centuries have taken the memorial far from its original site.*

The Tristan Stone

◆
Cornwall

Beside the road leading to Fowey in Cornwall stands an ancient, weathered stone measuring some 2 m (7 ft) in height and set in a concrete base. It was once much closer to Castle Dore (see page 52) and may have been the origin of the association of this site with the story of the tragic love of Tristan and Iseult. There is a Latin inscription on the stone, now much worn, which can be restored with only a little judicial guesswork to read:

Drustans hic iacet Cunomori filius

This means:

Drustanus lies here, the son of Cunomorus

It has been suggested, plausibly, that the characters referred to are Tristan, the son of Mark – Drustan being a recognized variant of the hero's name and Cunomorus being a Latinization of Cynvawr. Cynvawr, in turn, is said by the ninth-century author Nennius, who compiled the best historical account of Arthur, to be identified with Mark, the husband of Iseult.

▲ *Tristan, as well as being Iseult's lover, was one of the great heroes of the Round Table. Originally a separate story, his life became part of the great cycle of knightly adventures compiled during the Middle Ages.*

Maiden Castle

◆

Dorset

Among the many sites associated with the story of Tristan and Iseult is Maiden Castle, an Iron-Age fortress in the south-western corner of Dorset. Like Castle Dore (see page 52), it has been suggested as a possible site for the headquarters of King Mark, though, since he is nearly always described as the King of Cornwall, this may be a less likely ascription. Maiden Castle itself is a formidable series of banks and ditches, rising to more than 24 m (80 ft) in places and enclosing a huge area of land within its 3-km (2-mile) perimeter. Archaeological evidence suggests it was occupied from 300 BC onwards and, like several other such hill-forts, it was re-fortified during the period of Arthur's ascendancy, in the sixth century.

◀ *The massive banks and ditches of Maiden Castle would have proved virtually impregnable to attackers, who would have been perfect targets for spears and boulders thrown down from the wooden ramparts.*

The Round Table

◆

Winchester, Hampshire

◄ *The design currently displayed on the Winchester Round Table dates from 1552 and was made to impress the visiting Emperor Charles V. It depicts 24 places, named after the greatest of Arthur's knights. The topmost place is reserved for the king himself, though the likeness is actually that of Henry VIII, and a Tudor rose has been added at the centre as a reminder of the claims made by the Tudor dynasty of descent from Arthur.*

Accounts differ about the origin of the Round Table, at which Arthur's knights met to tell of their deeds and from which they invariably set forth in search of further adventures. The Norman chronicler Wace was the first to mention it, in his *Roman de Brut* of 1155. There, he simply says that Arthur devised the idea of a round table to prevent quarrels between his barons over the question of precedence. Another writer, Layamon, adapted Wace's account and added to it, describing a quarrel between Arthur's lords which was settled by a Cornish carpenter who, on hearing of the problem, created a portable table which could seat 1,600 men. Both Wace and Layamon refer to Breton story-tellers as their source for this and there is little reason to doubt them. This being the case, the origins of the table may well date back to Celtic times, and even be traceable to the age of Arthur himself. In the later medieval stories, however, it is Merlin who is responsible for the creation of the table. Malory, taking up the theme and developing it, made it the centre-piece of his epic re-telling.

The large wooden table in the Great Hall at Winchester dates from no earlier than the thirteenth century, when it may have been made at the command of King Edward III, who was considering a revival of the Round Table as an order of chivalry. In the end, he dropped this idea and created the Order of the Garter instead, but the table remains. Made of oak, it is 5.5 m (18 ft) across and nearly 8 cm (3 in) thick. It weighs nearly 1.25 tonnes.

▲ *These fine stained-glass windows at the western end of the Great Hall, depict three great kings: Alfred, Arthur and Cnut. Arthur has place of honour at the centre. The two Saxon monarchs are on either side of the great British king who did so much to keep the Saxons out of Britain!*

Bamburgh Castle

◆

Northumberland

Towering above the tiny village of Bamburgh on the bare, sandy coastline of Northumberland, the massive walls of this medieval fortress are one of two such places believed to be the original site of Lancelot's castle of Joyous Garde. Interestingly, there was a Dark-Age stronghold on the same site, which may account for this tradition. In 547 it became the capital of the Northumbrian 'kingdom' of the Angles who had settled there in the early part of the sixth century; as such, it would have been a stronghold of the Saxon alliance, who were Arthur's prime enemies in his fight to maintain British rule. At the time, the site was not called Bamburgh, but seems to have been named 'Din Guayrdi', which may have suggested Joyous Garde to Sir Thomas Malory, who first described it as Lancelot's holding in his fifteenth century Arthurian 'novel', *La Morte d'Arthur*.

◀ *This may be the site of Sir Lancelot's famous castle of Joyous Garde, where he once gave refuge to the runaway lovers, Tristan and Iseult, and where he himself retired to escape the rumours of his liaison with Arthur's queen.*

Alnwick Castle

◆

Northumberland

Alnwick is the second of two possible sites for Lancelot's castle of Joyous Garde, the other being Bamburgh Castle (see page 67), a little way further down the windswept coast of Northumberland. Sir Thomas Malory, in his great Arthurian romance *Le Morte d'Arthur*, mentions both: 'Some men say it was Anwick and some men say it was Bamborow.' The present castle dates from the eleventh century and, like its neighbouring fortress, it was first settled by the Angles around the middle of the sixth century. If it was fortified before then, no sign of that occupation now remains.

On the whole, the suggestion of Bamburgh as the original site of Lancelot's home seems more plausible, although, since Lancelot was meant to have been a native of France, neither place seems particularly appropriate as anything more than a temporary base. A more interesting, recent Arthurian association is that the American author John Steinbeck decided to write a new version of Malory's great book for twentieth-century readers while staying in the present castle (the home of the Duke of Northumberland). He spent a total of 20 years working on this massive undertaking, which gradually grew to have less and less to do with Malory. Unfortunately, Steinbeck died before the work was completed, though the first two-thirds were published after his death in 1968 as *The Acts of King Arthur and His Noble Knights* (Hodder & Stoughton, 1977).

Wetton Mill

◆

Staffordshire

In the great fourteenth-century poem *Sir Gawain and the Green Knight*, the hero encounters a fearsome figure with green skin, red eyes, and green clothing, who carries a great axe, and rides a green horse. This is the Green Knight, a spirit of winter and of the Otherworld, who offers a dreadful challenge to Arthur and his knights: to strike a blow with his axe which will be returned in a year. Gawain cuts off the Green Knight's head, only to see him pick it up and to hear the mouth speak words, calling him to a return match at the Green Chapel a year later.

More than one attempt has been made to identify the site of this mysterious chapel, which in the poem is no stone building but a cave amid deeply cracked rocks. One of the most convincing is Wetton Mill, also known as Nan Tor or Thurshole. It lies near the old Roman city of Chester, on the Staffordshire moorland, where Hoo Brook runs into the River Manifold. Its local name associates it with the Norse god Thor rather than the Green Knight, but this is certainly a later addition. The scholar Mabel Day was the first to point out the similarity between the description of the Green Chapel in the poem and this actual site. The poem was almost certainly composed in the area, and it is likely that the author knew Wetton.

▶ *It is easy to imagine the fearsome Green Knight of Arthurian tradition emerging from amid the rocks surrounding this cave.*

The King's Knot

◆

Stirling, Scotland

Lying in a field below the walls of Stirling Castle is the King's Knot, otherwise known, in local tradition, as King Arthur's Round Table. The Knot is really a series of interlinked earthworks, and it is octagonal rather than round, though there is a mound measuring about 12 to 15 m (40 to 50 ft) across at the centre. It appears to be the last remaining vestige of a formal garden dating from around 1627. It may be a memory from an earlier use of the site for one of the medieval chivalric entertainments which were commonly known as 'Round Tables'. The French writer Beroul, who wrote one of the earliest versions of the Tristan legend, mentions a stone slab kept at Stirling around which Arthur and the knights used to meet. No trace of this exists, and it is likely that it was a piece of local mythology designed to attract medieval tourists. However, the chronicler William of Worcester, writing in 1478, says 'King Arthur kept the Round Table at Stirling Castle'.

3

ARTHUR'S LAND

In olden days of the King Arthur,
Of which that Bretons speke great honour,
All was this land full of faerie.

Chaucer

AT the heart of Arthur's Britain are the sites associated with his name – many more than are pictured here. Some, like Freeborough Hill in Yorkshire or the 3 m (10 ft) high basalt pillar called Arthur's Chair nearby, have vanished for ever beneath the ploughs of farmers or the concrete wastelands of our cities. (For example, Wychbury Hill, near Kidderminster in the West Midlands, which was believed by some to be a contender for Arthurian associations, recently fell victim to a new road.) Many more have, thankfully, survived.

However, it is the places where Arthur is believed to have fought and defeated the invading Saxons which have left the deepest impression on the folk-memory of Britain. Recently, new evidence has been put forward suggesting that one of the contributory sources to the developing legend of Arthur may have been a contingent of Sarmatian cavalry stationed at Ribchester, near York (see *From Scythia to Camelot* by C. Scott Littleton and Linda A. Malcor). These warriors, originally from the steppes of Russia, among other things worshipped a sword stuck in a stone, and told stories of a quest for a mystical cauldron. Most importantly, however, they were skilled horsemen, and, it has been suggested, this was Arthur's greatest weapon against the Saxons. As long ago as 1932, historians R. G. Collingwood and

J. N. L. Myers, in *Roman Britain and the English Settlements* (Clarendon Press, 1936), suggested that cavalry was the secret of Arthur's success against the invaders. The Celtic tribes of the period did not have mounted fighters, but the use of mail-clad horsemen (a revival of methods used originally by the Romans) may well have turned the tide in favour of the Britons. This might well explain the extraordinary proliferation of sites where Arthur's twelve battles against the Saxons were supposedly fought. These are listed in the writings of the ninth-century monk Nennius, who gathered together a mass of fragmentary documents relating to the period of Arthur's activity. The battles are given as follows:

Then Arthur and the British kings fought the Saxons. He was their *dux bellorum* [duke of battles]. First he fought a battle at the mouth of the river Glein. He fought four others, on the river Dubglas in the region of Linnus. The sixth battle took place on the river called Bassus. The seventh was in the forest of Celidon, the Cat Coit Celidon. The eighth was the battle in the fort of Guinnion, in which Arthur bore the image of the Virgin on his shoulders. The pagans were put to flight that day and many of them were slaughtered, thanks to our lord Jesus Christ and the Blessed Virgin. A ninth battle took place at the City of Legions, a tenth on the banks of the river Tribruit. The eleventh on a mountain called Agned or Cat Bregouin. The twelfth battle took place at

◆ Previous page: *Llyn Barfog, Wales.*

Mount Badon, in which a single assault from Arthur killed 960 men and no other took part in this massacre. And in all these battles he was victor.

trans. J. Morris

This list has given more trouble to would-be chroniclers of the Arthurian period than almost any other. The names are unfamiliar, and their identification cannot be proved beyond a doubt. The best guess by modern historians and archaeologists would suggest that the Battle of Glein probably took place at or near the River Glen in Northumberland. The second, third, fourth and fifth battles were perhaps fought on or close to the River Douglas, in Scotland, which is only 5 km (3 miles) from the area known today as Lennox. Battle number six, on the River Bassus, is placed at Cambuslang, near modern-day Stirling. The seventh battle, at Cat Coit Celidon, has long been recognized as being fought in the area once occupied by the ancient Caledonian forest, possibly at the meeting-place of the borders between Peebles, Lanark and Dumfries. A Roman road crosses the mountains here, making it a good place for a skirmish. The eighth battle, at Guinnion, is tentatively identified with

Land's End. The ninth battle, specified as being fought at the City of the Legions (see page 86), probably took place in or near the modern city of Chester. For the tenth and eleventh battles, which according to Nennius were fought at the River Tribruit and at Mount Agned, the suggestions are Brent Knoll for the hill and the nearby area of sands known as Eirther Serts Flats or Berrow Flats for Tribruit. The twelfth and final battle, which set Arthur's star at its zenith, was fought at Nennius's 'Mons Badonicus', or 'the Mount near to Badon'. Again, numerous attempts have been made to identify this site, mostly without success. The best suggestion to date, which fits the few fragments of evidence available, places it near the Roman city of Bath, perhaps on Little Solsbury Hill or at Liddington hill fort – thought to be Arthur's stronghold.

Many of these sites possess little or no worth for a pictorial record of Arthur's presence. Hence, we have tried to assemble some of those which not only claim Arthurian association but are also, of themselves, evocative places which call to mind those far-off days when Arthur – king or hero, however we would wish to remember him – rode the land and left his impression upon it for ever.

▶ *One of the oldest surviving poems in Welsh,* The Gododdin, *describes a battle fought against the Angles by a band of warriors who hailed from 'Din Eydin', which is believed to be Edinburgh. Another poem of the same period speaks of Arthur and his men fighting 'on Eidyn's mountain'. This suggests a much earlier association, almost contemporaneous with Arthur.*

Arthur's Seat

◆

Edinburgh, Scotland

This huge crag, which rises to a height of 250 m (822 ft) above sea-level above the city of Edinburgh, has been known as Arthur's Seat since the fifteenth century. Part of Holyrood Park, it offers a tremendous view of the surrounding country and of the sea to the east. The 'seat' itself is said to be the notch between the highest point of the peak and a secondary point a little way to the south. In fact, it is probably named after a local hero who happened to bear the name Arthur. Interestingly enough, Edinburgh is identified with the Castle of Maidens in several Arthurian tales, which is probably because one of its medieval names was *Castellum Puellarum* (Castle of Women). In the stories it is sometimes a place where a number of female prisoners are kept; at other times it seems to be occupied by seductive women who tempt knights passing by. In at least one version, Arthur's half sister, the renowned 'enchantress' Morgan le Fay, is its mistress.

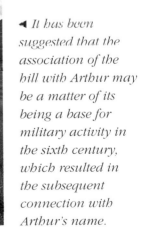

◀ *It has been suggested that the association of the hill with Arthur may be a matter of its being a base for military activity in the sixth century, which resulted in the subsequent connection with Arthur's name.*

Badbury Rings

◆

Dorset

This Iron-Age hill-fort has long been among the contenders for the site of Arthur's greatest battle against the Saxons – Badon Hill. The claim is based primarily on the similarity in the names, but there is also a degree of incidental evidence supported by its strategic importance and the fact that it was, like Cadbury and Castle Dore, re-fortified during the Arthurian period. Others argue that it was too far west to be the site of an important battle between the Saxons and the British, because the Saxons rarely, if ever, came this far inland at this point in time. However, they, like their British opponents, were perfectly capable of long marches. Badbury had yet to be excavated, so it remains an uncertain contender for the battle. The current site has beautiful views for most of its 7 ha (18 acres), and it is a favourite spot for weekend walkers.

The Battle of Badon was certainly a crucial one – the last of twelve encounters listed by the ninth-century chronicler Nennius as being fought under the leadership of Arthur. Badon essentially smashed the power of the Saxons for nearly 30 years, allowing them to become settlers rather than invaders and marking the beginning of the English race through the intermarriages which took place between Britons and Saxons during this period.

Arthur's Quoit

St David's Head, Wales

One of many prehistoric burial chambers which bear the name of Arthur. The one shown here is situated dramatically on St David's Head, overlooking the storm-tossed Atlantic. Whatever its original connections with local legend, it is part of a general trend throughout the lands once ruled by Arthur to remember him by naming significant, and especially sacred, sites after him.

▶ *In Cornish traditions particularly, Arthur is portrayed as a giant – much given to tossing stones or boulders of this kind about the landscape.*

Ogof Arthur

◆

Anglesey, North Wales

This is perhaps one of the most mysterious and frustrating of the many sites in this area which bear Arthur's name. Here, according to local legend, he sheltered during his war with the Irish pirates, known as *Gwyddelod*; and here, too, perhaps, he left a treasure. However, where is the cave where these events took place? Its entrance lies somewhere in the shadow of the cliffs on the south-western coastline of Anglesey, and it is said that it stretches a mile underground. Yet, the entrance is hidden by the tide, and the footing is treacherous even when the sea is out. Although some researchers claim that access to the cave is possible at low tide, local people say that the tide never goes out that far! It is possible that there may be a way through from the ancient burial chamber of Barclodiad y Gawres, which is on the cliffs above the cave.

The most interesting fact about this site is the reference to Arthur's battle with the Irish pirates. This may refer to a long-drawn-out and bitter struggle which supposedly took place between Arthur and the Sons of Caw, one of whom was the sixth-century chronicler Gildas. When he heard that Arthur had caught and hung his brothers, Gildas destroyed the book he was writing about Arthur and omitted the great warrior's name from all his subsequent work.

▲ *Here among the rocks and water is believed to lie the entrance to King Arthur's Cave. Its treasure – if treasure there is – remains beyond the reach of even the hardiest seeker.*

Caerleon-Upon-Usk

◆

Gwent, Wales

According to Geoffrey of Monmouth's twelfth-century *History of the Kings of Britain*, this was Arthur's chief city. In a lengthy description, it is made to rival the later Camelot in its splendour. It contained two minster churches where choirs sang praises to God non-stop, and a college of 200 scholars skilled in the arts of astrology and prediction. This is where Arthur was crowned and held his first court, presiding over a rich company including liveried knights and their ladies.

The present site contains the ruins of a fine Roman amphitheatre and extensive buildings, including bath houses and barracks. Until recent times, the central mound of the amphitheatre was called 'The Round Table'. Geoffrey's account probably lies behind this identification, and it was almost certainly prompted by his own patriotism – Monmouth, where Geoffrey was born, lies only a little way to the north. The town's Roman name, City of the Legions (Caer-Leon) led to its identification as the possible site of the ninth of the twelve great battles fought between Arthur and the Saxons.

▼ *Here, where once captives were marched into the amphitheatre to fight for the entertainment of Roman dignitaries, the Round Table was believed to have stood – the starting-point, in its turn, of many a knightly adventure.*

Llyn Barfog

◆

Gwynedd, Wales

◄ *Carn March Arthur, the Stone of Arthur's Horse.*

Llyn Barfog, or the Bearded Lake, is the setting for one of the most colourful of local stories about Arthur. It is said that a terrible monster, the *avanc*, lived in the lake, from where it would raid the surrounding countryside. When Arthur came to hear of this, he went to the lake and threw a great chain around the *avanc*. Then, with the help of his mighty horse (sometimes called Llamrai), he hauled the creature from the lake and killed it. Proof of this is found a short distance from Llyn Barfog in the shape of a stone known as Carn March Arthur, the Stone of Arthur's Horse. Here there is an undoubted hoof-print etched deeply into the rock – supposedly made by Arthur's steed as it strained to pull the *avanc* from the lake. No one knows exactly what the *avanc* looked like; it has been variously described as a dragon, a crocodile and a beaver. Judging from the size of the lake now, the latter would be its most likely inhabitant; no doubt, though, the lake was once much bigger.

Richmond Castle

◆

Yorkshire

On the hill overlooking the market town of Richmond stands the ruins of a Norman castle, believed to have once contained the entrance to an underground chamber in which Arthur and his knights lay sleeping. A local potter, named Thompson, is said to have found his way in and discovered the king and his men, together with a sword and a horn. He picked up the horn, and the sleepers began to stir. As potter Thompson fled in terror, a voice called out after him:

> Potter Thompson, Potter Thompson!
> If thou hadst drawn the sword or
> blown the horn,
> Thou hadst been the luckiest man
> e'er born!

This is almost exactly the same as the story about Sewingshields (see page 93) and Alderley Edge (see page 36). Richmond, however, is unusual in that another story mentions a secret passage leading from the hill to the nearby abbey of Easby. Here, it is said, a company of soldiers stumbled upon the entrance and sent a drummer boy in to explore it, while they went above ground, listening for the tap of his drum. Soon, the drumming stopped and nothing more was ever seen of the drummer, though it is said that his drum can sometimes still be heard coming from within the ground. The novelist William Mayne makes a wonderful story of this in *Earthfasts* (Hamish Hamilton, 1986), and potter Thompson's story was the subject of an opera by Humphrey Searl, with a libretto by Alan Garner.

Sewingshields Crag

◆

Northumberland

Sewingshields Crag and its two neighbouring peaks, King's Crags and Queen's Crags, are the focus for several stories concerning Arthur. Sewingshields itself is the site of another Arthurian cave myth (see also Alderley Edge, page 36, and Richmond Castle, page 90). A farmer accidentally found his way into a cavern below the peak where Arthur, Guinevere and their men lay asleep. A horn, a sheathed stone sword and a garter lay on a table. The farmer drew the sword, cut the garter, then placed the sword back in its sheath. At this point, Arthur awoke and said:

▼ *One of the finest stretches of Hadrian's Wall stands along the line of Sewingshields Crag. The place is associated with many Arthurian traditions.*

> *O woe betide that evil day*
> *On which this witless wight was born,*
> *Who drew the sword, the garter cut,*
> *But never blew the bugle-horn.*

He then fell asleep again as the frightened farmer fled. Apparently, the correct procedure would have been to draw the sword (no mean feat if it were really made of stone), cut the garter and blow the horn. Then, presumably, Arthur and all his followers would have awoken, but, as in all the stories in which Arthur is asleep beneath the hills, something always prevents him from awakening – until the right time.

Of King's and Queen's Crags, it is said that a giant Arthur and Guinevere once rested there and quarrelled. Arthur, in exasperation, threw a boulder at his queen, who deflected it with a comb. The boulder still lies between the two peaks, with the marks of the comb on it.

A third story concerns Arthur's sons, who are rarely mentioned in any of the romances. It tells the grim tale of the king's sojourn at the castle of the Seven Shields, where he was visited by a northern vassal. The chieftain was given gifts to take away, but the king's sons thought them too valuable and, having followed him to Cumming's Cross (a standing stone about 3 km/2 miles from the crags), they murdered him and took the gifts. This is one of a handful of stories which present Arthur and his kin in a less attractive light than usual.

Cerrig Meibion Arthur

◆

Gwynedd, Wales

These two standing stones, known locally as the 'Stones of the Sons of Arthur', stand in a valley among the Prescelly Mountains – where the famous blue-stones used in the construction of phase one of Stonehenge were quarried. Nothing is known of the story behind this name, and the stones themselves are clearly much older than the sixth century. References to Arthur's sons are rare indeed, though he has at least two who are mentioned by name in the medieval romances: Llacheu or Lohot, and Anir or Amr. Perhaps there was a legend concerning their deaths connected to this spot.

◄ *These two standing stones may mark the graves of two of Arthur's sons, though there are other places which claim this honour.*

Maen Chwyf

◆

Anglesey, North Wales

Also known as Arthur's Quoit, this massive stone is one of a number of such natural features which have been chosen as evidence of Arthur's prodigious strength. 'Arthur's Stones' are found as widely separated as Hereford, Reynoldstone, West Glamorgan, Llanafan in Dyfed, and Coupar Angus in Tayside. Most of them are the focus of local legends, in which Arthur appears as a giant and either engages in some rough sport in which huge boulders are tossed about, or finds a stone in his shoe and flings it away. This particular boulder was once known as a 'rocking' stone: balanced on several smaller rocks in such a way that it could be rocked by an individual. This is certainly no longer the case, because the stone had to be cleared of overgrowth before this photograph could be taken. Any original legendary connection with Arthur has not survived.

Cors-Y-Gedol

◆

Gwynedd, Wales

Also known as Arthur's Quoit, this site is actually the remains of a Stone-Age burial chamber. Local legend tells that when excavators come to investigate the site in the nineteenth century a local man predicted that bad weather would be the result. He was proved right, though it is not recorded whether the archaeologists gave up and went home as a result. There is a further tradition of buried treasure, though no sign of it has ever been found.

◄ *Buried treasure is said to lie beneath these stones, though nothing came to light when the site was excavated in the 1930s.*

Trethevy Quoit

Cornwall

In reality, this is a megalithic burial chamber, dating from the second millennium BC, yet this has not prevented it from acquiring Arthurian associations. The capstone, which measures some 3.75 m (12 ft) and weighs several tonnes, is called Arthur's Quoit, though it is unlike the majority of such stones supposedly thrown down by a gigantic form of the hero. At one time, the whole site would have been covered by a mound, and might therefore have been viewed as a 'fairy hill' by the local people. This mound, however, has long since eroded away, leaving the upright stones, capped by the huge 'quoit', standing alone in the middle of a field. Perhaps Arthur's well-known links with the fairy folk prompted the identification, but, whatever the truth, the Trethevy Quoit remains another enigmatic memorial to the hero who left so powerful a stamp on the land over which he ruled.

◀ ▲ *A mute testimony to the continuing fame of Arthur, Trethevy Quoit may once have possessed a story which connected it to some deed or battle in which the great hero took part. Whatever this was, it is no longer remembered today.*

Chapel Point

◆

Cornwall

Forming the southern tip of Mevagissy Bay is a long spit of land which stretches out into the sea. Here, according to local legend, Tristan made his famous leap to freedom after being captured by King Mark and sentenced to death for his adultery with Iseult, Mark's queen. The medieval French story-teller Beroul wrote of this in his twelfth-century romance, *Tristan and Yseult*. According to him, Tristan was to be burned at the stake, but on the way to the pyre he persuaded his guards to allow him to enter a chapel to pray. Once inside, Tristan barricaded the door and then leapt to safety from a window overlooking the sea. He landed on a large flat rock, ever after known as 'Tristan's Leap'. Whether or not Chapel Point is the exact spot is open to argument, especially as there is no longer any trace of a building there. The site known as Roche Rock (see page 55) is also claimed as the place where Tristan leaped. Curiously, very close to Chapel Point, another, much later, renegade, Sir Henry Bodrugan, is believed to have leapt from the cliffs on his horse and ridden into the sea while escaping from the soldiers of Henry VII after the failure of Lambert Simnel's rebellion in 1487.

4

THE GRAIL
AND THE
CAULDRON

The cup, the cup itself, from which our Lord
Drank at the last sad supper with his own.
This, from the blessed land of Aromat . . .
Aramathean Joseph, journeying brought
To Glastonbury, where the winter thorn
Blossoms at Christmas, mindful of our Lord.
And there awhile it bode, and if a man
Could touch or see it, he was healed at once,
By faith, of all his ills.

Alfred Tennyson

 NE of the central themes which threads itself through the tapestry of the Arthurian tradition is undoubtedly the Quest for the Grail. Once again, as is so often the case, the origins of the story begin in pre-Christian times with the search for a wonderful cauldron of knowledge and inspiration. The only surviving account of this comes from a poem, attributed to the sixth-century Welsh bard Taliesin, but not copied down until the ninth century. This poem, called 'The Spoils of the Otherworld', describes a voyage to seven islands, each one offering a different challenge leading eventually to the place where the cauldron is kept. The poem is obscure and it is not clear whether or not the undertaking is successful. Here are some lines from the beginning of the poem which set the scene:

In Caer Siddi Gwair's prison was
    readied,
As Pwyll and Pryderi foretold.
None before went there save he,
Where the heavy chains bound him.
Before the spoiling of Annwn he sang
    forever
This eternal invocation of poets:
Save only seven, none returned from
    Caer Siddi.

Since my song resounded in the
    turning Caer,
I am pre-eminent. My first song

Was of the Cauldron itself.
Nine maidens kindled it with their
    breath –
Of what nature was it?
Pearls were about its rim,
It would not boil a coward's portion.
Lleminawg thrust his flashing sword
Deep within it;
And before dark gates, a light was
    lifted.
When we went with Arthur – a
    mighty labour –
Save only seven, none returned from
    Caer Fedwydd.

This sparked off a vast literature. In the eleventh century a French poet, Chrétien de Troyes, wrote *Story of the Grail*, which told how the young innocent Perceval searched for a wonderful object called a 'graal'. The poem became immensely influential and, since Chrétien died leaving it unfinished, several other writers attempted to complete it. Robert de Borron, writing at about the same time as Chrétien, created a new version drawing upon Christian apocryphal writings, and transformed the Grail story for ever by identifying it with the Cup of the Last Supper. From here on, the Grail became a central Christian symbol, and a number of works were written describing the many quests of the Knights of the Round Table in search of this mystical object.

The most famous of these was the great cycle of books called *The Vulgate*

◆ Previous page:
*Glastonbury Tor,
Somerset.*

Cycle, or sometimes *The Lancelot-Grail*. Collected by monks of the Cistercian Order, this huge work – running to eight volumes – constitutes the main source for the Grail story, covering as it does a vast tapestry of events and introducing several new characters, including the saintly knight, Sir Galahad, whose sole task was to solve the mystery of the Grail.

From this book, Sir Thomas Malory derived his own masterpiece, *Le Morte d'Arthur* (completed in 1485), in which he stripped away the theology which makes the French book hard reading today. The result was an extraordinary and powerful sequence of spiritual adventures, culminating in three knights, Galahad, Perceval and Bors, finding the Grail. Malory's description of the first appearance of the Grail at Camelot has never been bettered:

And then the king and all the estates went home unto Camelot . . . and every knight sat in his own place as they were tofore-hand. Then anon they heard cracking and crying of thunder, that them thought the place should all to-drive. In the midst of this blast entered a sunbeam more clearer by seven times than ever they saw . . . Then began every knight to behold other, and either saw other, by their seeming, fairer than ever they saw afore . . . Then there entered into the hall the Holy Grail, covered with white samite, but there was none might see it, nor who bare it. And there was the hall filled with good odours, and every knight had such meats and drinks as he best loved in the world.

Le Morte d'Arthur, Book XIII, Chapter 7

Sites associated with the Grail today centre in and around the small market town of Glastonbury in Somerset (see pages 109–119) which has become a modern place of pilgrimage for those in search of the mystical power of the Grail. Other, more ancient sites, such as Dinas Bran in Wales (see page 126) – believed by many to be one of the places with a strong association with the Cauldron – or St Nechtan's Kieve in Cornwall (see page 133), are less well known but no less powerful. Though much of the Grail quest took place in the realm of the Otherworld, its influence can still be felt and experienced at these sacred spots where the veil between the worlds is especially thin.

Glastonbury Abbey

◆

Somerset

Crouched in the lee of three hills, most notably the Tor (see page 113), the ruins of Glastonbury Abbey are all that remain of what was once the greatest monastic foundation and church in all of Britain, second only in wealth and size to Westminster. At the height of the Middle Ages it was a shrine second to none in Europe, considered by some to be as important as Rome itself.

Here, according to legend, came Joseph of Arimathea, the uncle of Jesus who gave up his tomb to house the body of his nephew. Later, Joseph was given the Holy Grail, that most mystical vessel which had been used to celebrate the Last Supper and the first Eucharist, and which caught some of the blood of the crucified Christ as he hung upon the cross. After the Resurrection, Joseph fled to Britain with the cup and founded the first Christian church on the ancient island of Ynys Witrin, sometimes known as the Glass Isle, or Avalon, better known today as Glastonbury.

Arthur's body was brought here to be buried. Today, a plaque marks the spot where, in 1191, his tomb was apparently uncovered by builders working on the restoration of the abbey after it had been almost destroyed by fire in 1184. Whether this was truly Arthur's grave or a complicated forgery perpetrated by the monks to raise funds to rebuild their half-burned church has been contested ever since. A lead cross, last seen by William Camden in the eighteenth century, used to be displayed in the abbey. It read:

Here lies buried the renowned King Arthur
in the Isle of Avalon.

There are those who believe it a forgery and those who think it was the genuine gravestone of Britain's greatest king.

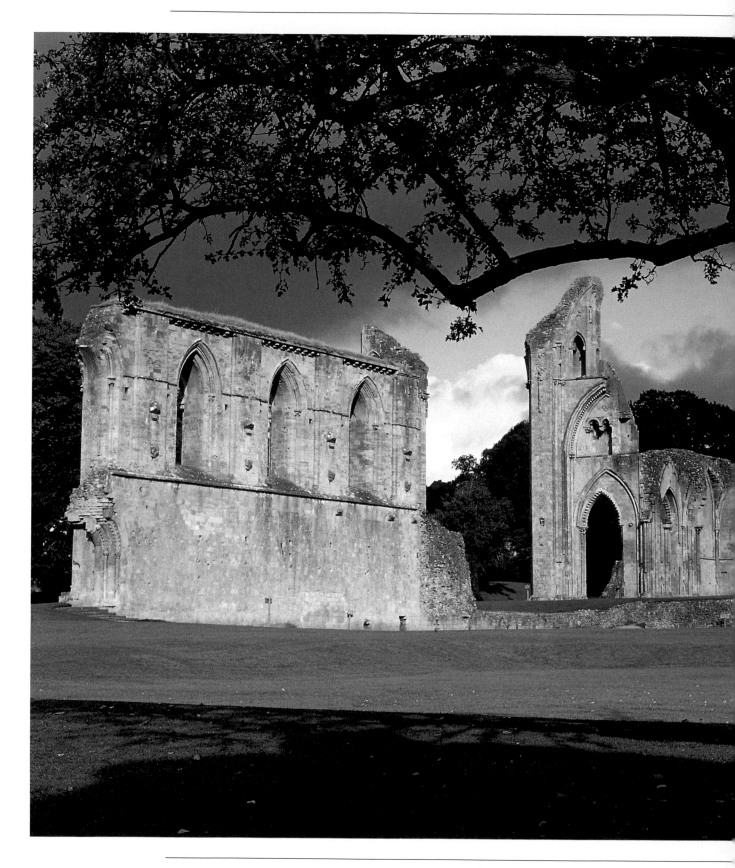

◄ *All that remains of the once mighty nave – the longest in Britain – partially destroyed in 1539 and subsequently mutilated to provide stones for walls and roads in the area.*

▼ *Here, according to legend, once lay the body of King Arthur. Discovered by accident in 1191, the bones – said to be larger than a normal man's – were re-interred in a black marble tomb on 19th April 1278 which was later destroyed – along with much of the abbey's treasure – when Henry VIII dissolved the foundation in 1539.*

SITE OF KING ARTHUR'S TOMB.
IN THE YEAR 1191 THE BODIES OF
KING ARTHUR AND HIS QUEEN WERE
SAID TO HAVE BEEN FOUND ON THE
SOUTH SIDE OF THE LADY CHAPEL.
ON 19TH APRIL 1278 THEIR REMAINS WERE
REMOVED IN THE PRESENCE OF
KING EDWARD I AND QUEEN ELEANOR
TO A BLACK MARBLE TOMB ON THIS SITE.
THIS TOMB SURVIVED UNTIL THE
DISSOLUTION OF THE ABBEY IN 1539

Glastonbury Tor

◆

Somerset

Rising like a beacon from the flat Somerset plain, the Tor seems to beckon the pilgrims who journey in their thousands to this remarkable spot, once described as 'this holiest earth'. People come in search of many things: the Grail; enlightenment; inspiration. Many claim to have found their goal, and remain in the peaceful market town to the bewilderment of the local inhabitants. Beneath the Tor is said to lie a subterranean kingdom ruled over by the Lord of the Wild Hunt, Gwynn ap Nud, a powerful other-worldly figure who was once banished by the Celtic St Collen, but who is still believed to haunt the hills around Glastonbury. A recent theory claims the existence of a man-made, sevenfold maze, carved out of the Tor itself. This, it is said, was once a sacred processional way, used by priests and priestesses to reach the stone circle which then crowned the Tor. Modern pilgrims still trace its path to the summit and speak of visionary experiences when they have done so.

From the summit of the Tor, which rises some 150 m (500 ft) above sea-level, there is a panoramic view of the surrounding countryside. Cadbury Castle (see page 50) can be glimpsed away to the south, and Brent Knoll rises away to the west, near the Bristol Channel. The Tor was probably once an island, hence its identification with the mysterious Island of Avalon, a place between the worlds, where tradition says that Arthur came to be healed of his wounds and to await his recall in a time of great need. This is the most likely reason for the legend of his grave being found in the abbey ruins below the hill.

▶ *On top of the Tor stands the tower of the church of St Michael, all that remains of a later building which replaced a still earlier medieval church which was destroyed by an earthquake in the thirteenth century.*

◀ *Glimpsed from afar, across the flat Somerset plain, the Tor rises like a great beached whale, its terraced sides all that remain of a sacred route to the summit.*

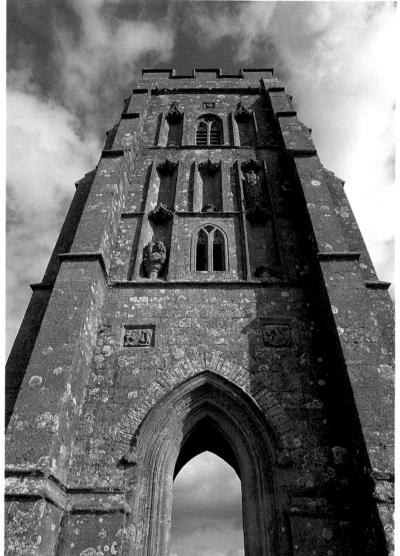

▲ High up on the side of the tower of St Michael is a carving representing St Bridget milking her cow. She is one of several famous Celtic saints – including St David and St Patrick – who may have lived for a time at Glastonbury.

◄ *Beneath the slopes of the Tor is said to lie a hidden cavern, once reached by a tunnel into the side of the hill. Nothing is now known of the tunnel, which was sealed in the early 1900s. Those who found their way within were believed to go mad.*

Wearyall Hill

◆

Glastonbury, Somerset

According to medieval tradition, Joseph of Arimathea came here with the sacred Christian relic of the Holy Grail. Arriving by ship nearby, Joseph walked inland and climbed the middle hill of which the Tor is the highest of the three. Weary after his long journey, he planted his staff, which promptly burst into leaf and flower. Thereafter, the hill was named Wearyall, and a scion of the original thorn tree (the product of Joseph's staff) may still be seen there today. Of the three hills, Wearyall has a special feeling of tranquillity.

▶ *This gentle hill offers a spectacular view of the Tor (see pages 112–115), from where you can see how easily it could become an island when the tidal waters rose across the Somerset Levels.*

Chalice Well Gardens

Glastonbury, Somerset

Chalice Hill is the third and gentlest of the three hills which form the heart of Glastonbury's sacred landscape. It stands between the town and the Tor, effectively hiding the bulk of the taller hill from the town. It has long been considered the most sacred of the hills, and it is believed by many to have been the final resting place of the Grail. A spring, rich in iron which turns the water red, rises here, and a peaceful garden has grown up around it in the past decade, owned and looked after by a local trust. Within the garden, which is surrounded by medieval stonework and rises up the lower slopes of the hill, there are a number of sheltered spots in which the visitor may stop and meditate or dream of the Grail and Arthur. The well-head is covered with an elaborate lid with a fine wrought-iron sculpture of the Vesica Pisces, a sign interpreted as representing the overlapping of the inner and outer worlds. Lower down, the waters spill out of a carved ornate fountain-head and fill a series of stepped bowls which echo the shape of the well-cover design. The reddish tinge to the water resulted in its once being called the Blood Spring; in modern times, it has been mystically associated with the blood of Christ caught in the Grail.

▲ *Water spills out of this lion-headed fountain into a shallow bowl. Pilgrims come to the fountain to drink the waters which are believed to possess healing qualities. They are rich in iron and have a clean taste which genuinely lifts the spirits.*

▶ *The well-head is covered by a wooden lid with a fine wrought-iron sculpture designed by Frederic Bligh-Bond, whose remarkable findings while excavating the abbey ruins were ridiculed when it was discovered he had used a psychic to trace the foundations of the ancient church.*

▶ *Here the reddish waters of the spring are channelled from the well-head above down into a wide and shallow basin shaped like two overlapping circles – an ancient, mysterious symbol dating from centuries before Glastonbury became a centre for pilgrims in search of the Grail.*

Lochmaben

◆

Dumfries and Galloway, Scotland

On the banks of this peaceful lake, the temple to the child-god Mabon or Maponus may once have been sited. Mabon was one of the major deities of the Celtic peoples. Somewhat akin to the Greek Apollo, he appears in the medieval Welsh story of 'Culhwch and Olwen', in which he is rescued from prison by Arthur's warriors. This story has been shown to contain the last traces of a very ancient mystery tale, concerning the loss and recovery of innocence.

The local story of Lochmaben is about another Celtic saint, Sampson, who was born here in the sixth century after his mother had a dream in which she was visited by an angel and told that she would bear a famous child. This may have been the reason for the association with Merlin, whose birth was similar; both Nikolai Tolstoy and Ean Begg have suggested that Merlin may have served at this temple, perhaps even becoming its resident prophet. A little to the south is a large circular earthwork, which was once known as King Arthur's Round Table. It may be the site of the original temple, though it does not seem to have ever been excavated (see also the Clochmabenstane, page 125).

The Clochmabenstane

◆

Dumfries, Scotland

This massive megalithic boulder, which now stands alone in a field near the Solway Firth, was probably once part of a larger circle of stones which may have been part of the central enclosure of a temple dedicated to the Celtic child-god Mabon. Like the nearby Lochmaben (see page 123), it recalls the story of the freeing of Mabon, by Arthur and his warriors from a mysterious castle in Wales. The tale is told in full in 'Culhwch and Olwen', one of the stories from the collection of Celtic myths known as *The Mabinogion*.

Here we learn how the heroic war-band of the island of Britain, helped by a series of magical creatures, each one older than the next, was able to free the enigmatic Mabon from centuries-long imprisonment in a cave beneath a no-longer identifiable castle somewhere in Wales.

Dinas Bran

◆

Glamorgan, Wales

Above the north side of the Vale of Llangollen rises the high and remote hill of Dinas Bran, named after the great Celtic god whose head was buried beneath the White Mount in London (now the site of the Tower of London), from where it kept watch over Britain and prevented invasion from across the Channel. Arthur ordered it dug up in the belief that he alone could defend the country. Despite his efforts, the Saxons did eventually overwhelm Britain.

On the brow of the hill stand the dramatic remains of a medieval castle. It is believed by some Arthurian scholars to be the original model for the castle of the Grail, the mysterious fortress to which the Knights of the Round Table came in search of the holy relic. This is interesting, since Bran, who was wounded in the thigh by a poisoned spear, may have been the origin of the mysterious Fisher King, the Grail's guardian, who suffered a similar wound. The thirteenth-century romance *Perlesvaus*, or *The High History of the Holy Grail*, mentions Dinas Bran in terms which lead one to suppose that it was recognized as the Grail castle. It is also said that a golden harp is hidden within the bulk of the mountain, and that only a boy who owns a white dog with silver eyes will find it.

▶ *The dramatic ruins of a medieval castle crown the heights of Dinas Bran. They stand on the site of a much earlier, Iron-Age fortress which could have been occupied in Arthur's day.*

▶ *Dinas Bran Castell, seen from across the beautiful Vale of Glamorgan. It is easy to see why it is associated with the mystery of the Grail castle, where adventures rich and strange awaited all who went there.*

St Michael's Mount

◆

Cornwall

Believed to mark the site of a great battle between Arthur and a local giant, this dramatic building rises above the sands of Mount's Bay, where tradition had it that Joseph of Arimathea used to come to ply his trade as a tin merchant. Joseph is later believed to have brought the sacred relic of the Holy Grail to Britain, and to have built the first Christian church at Glastonbury, in Somerset (see page 109). A firmly entrenched tradition says that he brought his young nephew, Jesus, with him on one of his many trips to Britain. Since biblical testimony is silent about the life of Jesus before his ministry, there could be some truth in this.

According to local legend, the hermit Ogrin, who lived at nearby Roche Rock (see page 55) brought about a brief reconciliation between the estranged King Mark and his Queen Iscult, who had been living in the wilds with her lover Tristan. Because the queen had only rags to wear, Ogrin bought fresh clothing and a horse for her at a fair on the Mount of St Michael.

◀ *At high tide the sea covers a causeway leading out to St Michael's Mount, effectively turning it into an island.*

◀ *According to
Geoffrey of
Monmouth, Arthur
stopped here on his
way to Gaul to fight
the Emperor of
Rome. During his
stay, he fought and
killed a giant. Local
tradition speaks
of such a being,
whose name was
Cormoran, though it
recalls nothing of
Arthur's part in his
demise.*

5

THE
LAST
BATTLE

O'er Cornwall's cliffs the tempest roar'd,
High the screaming sea-mew soar'd;
On Tintagel's topmost tower
Darksome fell the sheeting shower;
Round the rough Castle shrilly sung
The whirling blast, and wildly flung
On each tall rampart's thundering side
The surges of the tumbling tide;
When Arthur ranged his red cross ranks
On conscious Camlan's crimson banks.

Thomas Wharton

Lyonesse

◆

Cornwall

To stand on the tip of Land's End and look out towards the Isles of Scilly is to view all the remains of a once-thriving kingdom. It was named Lyonesse and tradition records that it was ruled over by Tristan's father. After his death, Tristan became heir to this rich land, but he was never to take up his inheritance, because Lyonesse sank beneath the sea while he was still at his uncle Mark's court in Cornwall. Numerous legends surround this wild promontory, including one that describes a local man, named Trevilian, who foresaw the disaster and, leaping on to his white horse, outran the advancing sea and took refuge in a cave near Marazion. From there, he watched Lyonesse disappear. The family coat of arms still bears a horse emerging from water.

Lyonesse has been variously identified with Lothian in Scotland – which was written in old French as Loonois – and with Leonais in Brittany, whereas in Cornwall it is called Lethowstow. It is one of several drowned lands – another being the Cantref Gwaelod which once lay where Cardigan Bay now stretches. The sixteenth-century antiquarian, William Camden, collected a number of stories from the local people, and recalls that they referred to the Seven Stones reef off Land's End as the City of Lions (Lyonesse). They also claimed to be able to hear the bells of the drowned city ringing out during rough seas, a story which is still current today. Certainly, if one takes a boat out on a calm day it is possible to catch a glimpse of walls beneath the water, and what are clearly the remains of field boundaries show up at low tide along the sands of the Sampson Flats between the isles of Tresco and Sampson.

Slaughter Bridge

◆

Cornwall

The mystery of Arthur's last resting place seems unlikely to be solved either now or in the future. An old Welsh poem, dating from a time when memory of the great war-leader was still fresh, says:

> *Not wise (the thought)*
> *A grave for Arthur.*

This has always seemed a clear enough imperative against trying to find a grave for a leader who went back into the land as mysteriously as he emerged from it. This has not stopped people from looking, of course, and there are a number of sites which claim this honour: one is the impressive 2.75 m (9 ft) long slab of stone, with a Latin inscription, lying on the banks of the River Camel some 180 m (200 yd) north of the modern Slaughter Bridge. The name of the bridge, and its connection with the Camel – which is believed by many to be the site of the Battle of Camlan, where Arthur received seemingly fatal wounds – caused antiquarians in the seventeenth and eighteenth centuries to think that this stone once marked Arthur's grave. With a little restoration, the inscription reads:

LATINICICIT FILIUSMAGARI

This was taken to read 'The monument of Atry'. However, this was a misreading of the rubbed and battered letters, which were certainly carved by someone with only a passing knowledge of Latin. Corrected, the inscription reads: *The Monument of Latinus: here lies the son of Magarus*, the last four letters of the name having provided the 'Atry' of earlier decipherments.

There is something moving about this monument, which now lies forgotten beneath some trees at the side of the river. It once stood in a nearby field which has long been considered the actual battle site, and as such might well be genuine – if not a memorial to Arthur himself, perhaps to one of his followers. Indeed, old bits of armour and swords were regularly found in and near the river in past times, though these could be accounted for by another battle, in 823, between the Saxons and the Cornish.

For a time, the stone formed an actual bridge across the river, until it was moved in the eighteenth century, when it was seen by the antiquarian William Camden, who also saw the cross at Glastonbury (see page 109) which was supposed to have marked Arthur's grave.

◄ Once believed to mark the grave of Arthur, this huge slab of stone is really a memorial to an unknown man named Magarus. Close by is the supposed site of the Battle of Camlan, where Arthur and his son Mordred mortally wounded each other, and where the river was said to have run red with the blood of the fallen.

The Eildon Hills have long been recognized as a centre of magic and mystery. They are the haunt of more than one unearthly figure, including the Scots wizard Michael Scott, who is attributed with splitting the hills into three. Another figure of whom many stories are told is Thomas Rhymer, whose conjectured dates are from 1220 to 1297. Apparently, he visited the fairy lands beneath Eildon and became the captive of the Fairy Queen for three years, during which time he learned the arts of prophecy. Both these figures are very like Merlin in character, and it is perhaps no surprise to find the story of the sleepers under the hill, also told of Alderley Edge (see page 36) and Sewingshields Crag (see page 93), as well as several other places.

The story is much the same in each case: a traveller is returning home and meets a stranger who offers him antique coin in payment for a horse. The traveller then finds himself invited into a huge underground cavern, where Arthur and his knights lie sleeping. The Eildon legend differs from the others in that the traveller is shown a sword and a horn, which he blows, waking the sleepers. He then draws the sword to protect himself. The stranger, who in this version is Thomas Rhymer himself, tells him that had he first drawn the sword and then blown the horn he would have become King of Britain.

The Eildon Hills

Roxburghshire, Scotland

▼ *Local tradition has Arthur and his knights sleeping beneath the Eildon Hills, awaiting the coming of a visitor who will draw a sword and blow a horn to wake them, before leading them in time of great need. Here, instead of Merlin, the traditional guardian of the sleepers, it is the local seer, Thomas Rhymer, who watches and waits for the fateful moment to arrive.*

Dozemary Pool

◆

Cornwall

◄ *Despite local legends, which describe this as the lake into which Sir Bedivere cast Arthur's magical sword, Excalibur, this seems no more than a nineteenth-century fabrication.*

Here, according to local tradition, Sir Bedivere finally threw away Arthur's famous magic sword, Excalibur. It took him three attempts, so drawn was he to the mighty weapon; when he finally complied with the wounded king's wish, a hand rose from the lake and caught the sword and brandished it three times before vanishing again beneath the water. In fact, this is one of several sites where this event is supposed to have taken place: Pomparles Bridge, at Glastonbury, is another, as is Looe Pool (see page 149) and Llyn Llydaw in Wales. In reality, despite its atmospheric setting high on Bodmin Moor, Dozemary is one of the least likely sites for the last resting place of Excalibur. For one thing, it is too far from any of the traditional sites of the Battle of Camlan, where Arthur received his fatal wound; for another, despite stories of the lake being bottomless, it is far from that and in fact dried up almost entirely in 1859, making it an unlikely home for the Lady of the Lake.

Looe Pool

◆

Cornwall

Though it is generally described as a lake, this stretch of water is really a lagoon, a long inlet of Mount's Bay, which is cut off from open water by Looe Bar, a ridge of stony sand extending out from the beach at Porthleven. Like Dozemary Pool (see page 147), it is one of the places claiming to be the last resting place of Arthur's magical sword, Excalibur. According to local legend, the last of Arthur's knights to survive the Battle of Camlan, Sir Bedivere, came here with instructions to throw the sword into the water. At first he was reluctant, thinking no doubt of the power which resided within the sword, as well as its beauty and richness. Three times he hid the sword and returned to the mortally wounded Arthur, who lay nearby, and reported that he had done as his king commanded. Each time when Arthur asked what he had seen, Bedivere answered, 'nothing but the water and the waves', at which Arthur sent him back again. Finally, Bedivere threw the sword as far as he could into the water, and saw an arm rise to catch and take it from sight.

◀ *There is some credence for the setting of this legend at Looe. The land is similar to the descriptions of the battle in the Arthurian romances, and it is possible for Arthur to have been taken away by sea from Mount's Bay, just as it was recounted in the stories, where three queens appear in a black draped barge to take him to Avalon. Certainly, Tennyson seems to have been thinking of this spot when he described the death of Arthur in his famous cycle of poems,* Idylls of the King.

Pentre Ifan

◆

Gwent, Wales

This constitutes one of the finest Bronze-Age burial chambers in Wales. Dating from somewhere between 4000 and 2000 BC, it is over 3 m (10 ft) high in places and dramatically placed on low-lying land near Newport. Local legends have given it the name 'Arthur's Quoit', thereby adding it to the collection of stones bearing this name – all probably stemming from a story about the giant Arthur (a figure who vanished long ago from the literature of the Arthurian heroes) either dropping or throwing a huge stone. The stones of Pentre Ifan (it is not certain which is the quoit) would once have been covered by an earth mound, beneath which the bones of the dead were laid.

▼ *Another of the numerous stones, scattered across the length and breadth of Britain, which bear the name of Arthur.*

King Arthur's Bed

◆

Cornwall

This huge granite monolith lies along a ridge of rocky outcrops on Bodmin Moor close to Hawk's Tor. Weathering has hollowed it into the appearance of a giant coffin – one reason why it has been described as Arthur's Bed. Local traditions suggest that it was either his grave or a bed hollowed out for Arthur – the kingly giant – who is so much a part of Cornish mythology.

▶ *'Not wise the thought, a grave for Arthur' – so runs the line of a sixth-century poem. This has not stopped people from seeking a resting place for the great hero among such giant stones as the one pictured here.*

GLOSSARY

◆

OF NAMES AND SUBJECTS

Amr or Anir: Name given to one of Arthur's sons.

Arfderydd: Famous, possibly historical battle during which Merlin went mad.

Arthur: Historical, sixth-century warrior who grew to become the great king of medieval myth and legend.

Avalon: Name of the magical island to which Arthur is taken to be healed of his wounds and to await his country's need in future times; sometimes identified with Glastonbury.

Bedivere: Arthur's butler and the last of his knights to survive the Battle of Camlan. Ordered to throw Excalibur into the lake, he took three attempts to do so.

Bran: Celtic god who was given the title 'Bendegied' (Blessed). He seems to have been the prototype of the wounded Fisher King.

Bridget: Celtic goddess who later became one of the patron saints of Ireland; believed to have stayed at Glastonbury.

Cadfan: Historical, sixth-century Breton prince.

Camlan: Name of the last battle where Arthur and Mordred met and gave each other mortal wounds.

Caw: Pirate chieftain killed by Arthur.

Collen: Sixth-century saint who faced Gwynn ap Nudd on Glastonbury Tor.

Cormoran: Cornish giant of St Michael's Mount killed by Arthur.

Culhwch: Celtic hero, who was also Arthur's nephew.

Cynfawr: Possibly the original name of King Mark.

David: Patron saint of Wales, believed to have stayed at Glastonbury.

Drustan: Alternative spelling of the name Tristan.

Emrys: Alternative name for Merlin, i.e., Myrddin Emrys or Merlin Ambrose.

Excalibur: Arthur's enchanted sword given to him by the Lady of the Lake.

Fergus of Galloway: Arthurian knight whose adventures take place in the area of Scotland containing sites strongly associated with Merlin.

Fisher King: The mysterious Guardian of the Grail in the medieval stories. He suffered an unhealing wound which could only be cured by finding the sacred vessel.

Galabes: Fountain named after a Celtic saint. Merlin was cured of his madness here.

Galahad: Saintly knight who found the Grail.

◀ *St Nechtan's Kieve, Cornwall. This Celtic saint is believed to have lived nearby in Arthurian times (AD c.500). A local legend claims it as the place from where the Grail Knights set out on their quest.*

INDEX OF SITES

◆

Photographs isolated from the text are indicated in italic.